D0820180

Florence Nightingale

By Carol Alexander

Consultant
Nanci R. Vargus, Ed.D.
Assistant Professor of Literacy
University of Indianapolis, Indianapolis, Indiana

Children's Press®
A Division of Scholastic Inc.
New York   Toronto   London   Auckland   Sydney
Mexico City   New Delhi   Hong Kong
Danbury, Connecticut

Designer: Herman Adler Design
Photo Researcher: Caroline Anderson
The photo on the cover shows Florence Nightingale.

Library of Congress Cataloging-in-Publication Data

Alexander, Carol.
  Florence Nightingale / by Carol Alexander; consultants Nanci R. Vargus.
    p. cm. — (Rookie biography)
  Includes bibliographical references and index.
  ISBN 0-516-24406-X (lib. bdg.)   0-516-25828-1 (pbk.)
  1. Nightingale, Florence, 1820-1910—Juvenile literature. 2. Nurses—
England—Biography—Juvenile literature. I. Vargus, Nanci Reginelli. II. Title.
III. Series.
  RT37.N5A455 2004
  610'.73'092—dc22

                                    2004000428

Do you think helping people get well is an important job?

Florence Nightingale did. She became a nurse. She proved that nurses are soldiers. They fight against disease.

Florence Nightingale

5

Florence Nightingale's home in England.

Nightingale was born on May 12, 1820, in Florence, Italy. She grew up in London, England.

Her family was rich. They did not understand why Nightingale wanted to be a nurse.

Nightingale believed she had a special job to do. She liked helping others. She liked taking care of sick people.

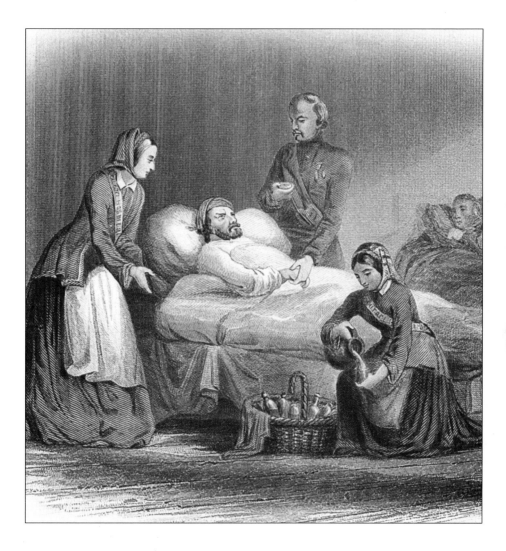

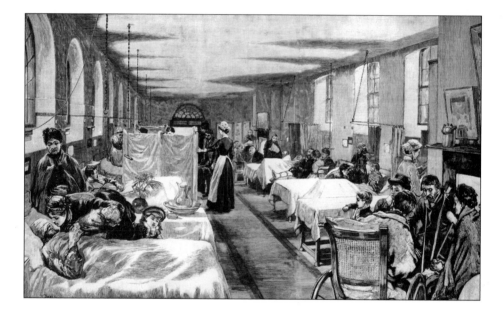

Nightingale's mother and father
did not want her to become
a nurse.

In those days, hospitals were dirty
places. Only poor people went
to hospitals.

In 1851, Nightingale studied nursing in Germany. Then she went to London to work at a women's hospital. She loved her work.

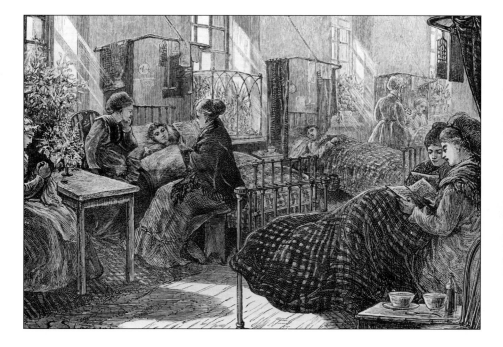

13

14

Nightingale had new ideas for helping sick people.

She gave them bells to ring when they needed help. She made sure they had clean, hot water for baths.

In 1854, there was a war. Nightingale was asked to be in charge of nursing sick soldiers. She and other nurses went to a hospital in Turkey.

18

The hospital was dirty. There were not enough beds or bandages for the soldiers.

Nightingale found men to clean the building. She wrote many reports and letters to ask for supplies.

Nightingale carried a lamp when
she worked in the hospital at night.

That is why the soldiers called her "the lady with the lamp." Soon, Nightingale became famous for her work.

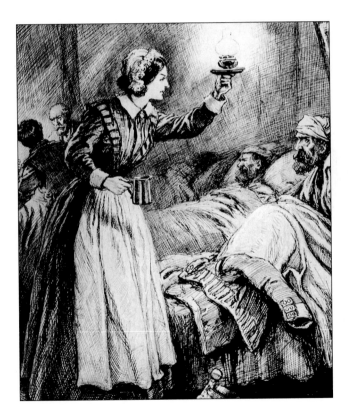

Nightingale worked where the battles were fought. She became very ill, but she would not stop working.

After the war, many people asked Nightingale for help.

She worked with the government to help make hospitals in Britain better. She also wrote many books and reports.

NOTES ON NURSING:

WHAT IT IS, AND WHAT IT IS NOT.

BY

FLORENCE NIGHTINGALE.

LONDON:
HARRISON, 59, PALL MALL,
BOOKSELLER TO THE QUEEN.

25

In 1860, Nightingale started a school for nurses.

Nurses from the school went to work in hospitals around the world.

Nightingale lived to be 90 years old. She helped change hospitals and health care around the world. She showed many people how to become nurses.

Today, we know that nurses make a difference in the lives of sick people.

A male nurse with his patient.

Words You Know

bandages

Florence Nightingale

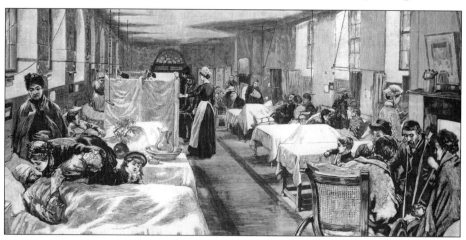

hospital

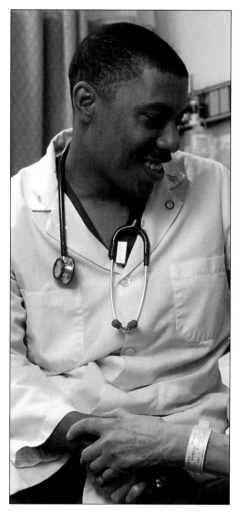

lamp

nurse

31

Index

About the Author

Carol Alexander has written both fiction and nonfiction for children and young adults. She has taught English in colleges around the New York City area. She lives in Manhattan with her husband and daughter.

Photo Credits